WEBSITE:
http://www.everra.com/store/glowing
SOCIAL MEDIA INFO
http://www.facebook.com/joyfully.jallah11

ISBN: 9798705421442

HOW TO OVERCOME
MENTAL HEALTH?
1. TAKE A SHOWER OR
BATH DAILY.
2. SEE A DOCTOR.
3. EXERCISE.
4. LOVE YOURSELF.
5. WRITE A JOURNAL OF
HOW YOU FEEL
DAILY.
6. PRAY & ASK GOD TO
HEAL YOUR SOUL.
7. DO WHAT YOU LOVE
DOING.

Introduction:

When a man is careful how he handles a woman, it reveals his love for her and love towards her. This book will encourage men how to care and love a woman. The gift God sent into man's life, truly a woman to help him fulfill his purpose.

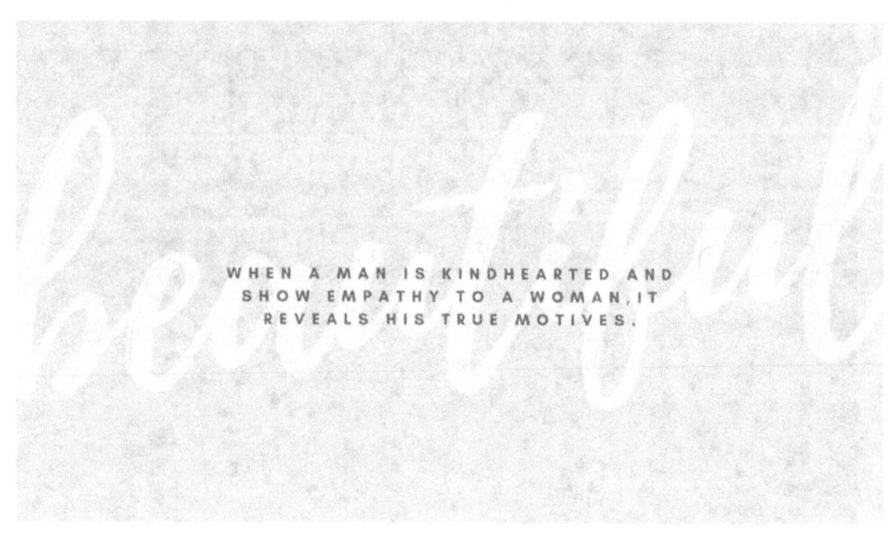

Gratitude Journal

____

____

____

____

How to cope with depression?

1. Journal how you feel everyday.
2. Take a bath or showers.
3. Invest in yourself into self development.
4. Have fun.
5. See a Doctor.

HOW CAN A MAN SHOW A WOMAN LOVE?

WHEN HE IS GENTLE SPOKEN TO HER, AND WHEN HE MAKES HER FEEL SAFE. WHEN HIS LOVE IS GENUINE. WHEN HE LISTENS TO HER. WHEN HE VALUES HER. WHEN HE APPRECIATES HER, AND SHOWS IT.

AFFIRMATION PRAYERS: HOLY SPIRIT WE DEPEND ON YOU. LET YOUR WILL BE DONE. LET YOUR KINGDOM COME ON EARTH AS IT IS IN HEAVEN.

DATE:
TIME:

Gratitude Journal

Gratitude Journal

DATE:
TIME:
GRATITUDE JOURNAL

____

____

____

____

Gratitude Journal

____

____

____

____

____

THERE IS HOPE.

FORGIVE.

See the best in everyone regardless of their behavior. When times are uncertain and difficult, keep pressing forward. Never give up. There is greatness ahead.

Gratitude Journal

____

____

____

____

____

____

WHAT IS TRUE LOVE?

-Caring for others.

-Thoughtful of others.

-Forgiving others.

Gratitude Journal

____

____

____

____

____

____

Date:
Time:
Gratitude
Journal

DATE:
TIME:
GRATITUDE JOURNAL

WHY ARE YOU GRATEFUL?

Date:
Time:
Gratitude
Journal

GRATITUDE JOURNAL

____

____

____

____

DATE:
TIME:

Gratitude Journal

____

____

____

____

DATE:
TIME:
GRATITUDE JOURNAL

Date:
Time:
GRATITUDE
JOURNAL

DATE:
TIME:
Gratitude
Journal

DATE:
TIME:
GRATUTUDE JOURNAL

Date:
Time:
Gratitude
Journal

Date:
Time:
Gratitude Journal

Date:

Time:

Gratitude Journal

____

____

____

____

DATE:
TIME:
Gratitude Journal

Date:
Time:
Gratitude Journal

Date:
Time:
Gratitude
Journal

Date:

Time:

Gratitude Journal

DATE:

TIME:

Gratitude Journal

____

____

DATE:
TIME:

Gratitude Journal

Love
Date:
Time:
Gratitude Journal

Date:
Time:
GRATITUDE JOURNAL

Date:

Time:

Gratitude Journal

Date:
Time:
Gratitude Journal

____
____
____
____

DATE:
TIME:
GRATITUDE
JOURNAL

Date:
Time:
Gratitude Journal

GRATITUDE
JOURNAL:
DATE:
TIME:

Date:
Time:
Gratitude
Journal

Date:

Time:

GRATITUDE JOURNAL

Date:
Time:
Gratitude Journal

DATE:
TIME:
Gratitude
Journal

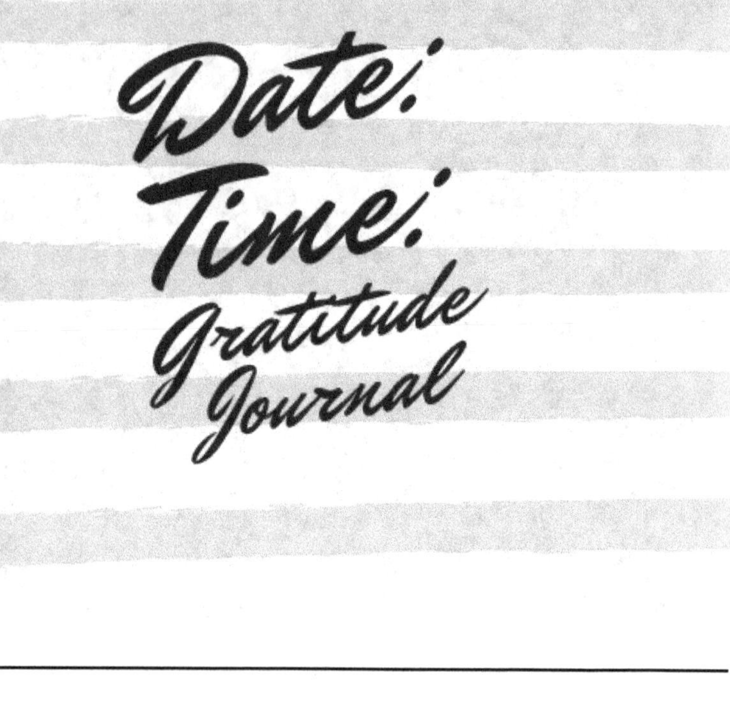
Date:
Time:
Gratitude
Journal

____

____

____

____

Date:

Time:

Gratitude Journal

Date:
Time:
Gratitude Journal

Date:
Time:
GRATITUDE JOURNAL

Date:
Time:
Gratitude Journal

Date:
Time:
Gratitude Journal

Date:
Time:
Gratitude Journal

Date:
Time:
Gratitude Journal

DATE:
TIME:

Gratitude Journal

DATE:
TIME:
Gratitude Journal

DATE:
TIME:

GRATITUDE JOURNAL

Date:
Time:
GRATITUDE JOURNAL

Date:
Time:
Gratitude Journal

DATE:
TIME:
GRATITUDE
JOURNAL

DATE:
TIME:
GRATITUDE
JOURNAL

DATE:
TIME:

Gratitude Journal

DATE:

TIME:

GRATITUDE JOURNAL

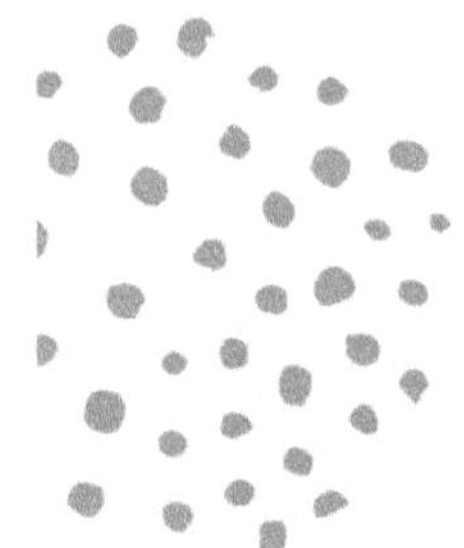

DATE:
TIME:
GRATITUDE JOURNAL

____

____

____

____

GRATITUDE JOURNAL

Date:
Time:

Gratitude Journal

____

____

____

____

Date:
Time:

Gratitude
Journal

____

____

____

____

Date:

Time:

Gratitude Journal

____

____

____

____

Date:
Time:
Gratitude Journal

____

____

____

____

Date:
Time:
Gratitude Journal

DATE:
TIME:
GRATITUDE JOURNAL

Date:
Time:
Gratitude Journey

DATE:
TIME:
GRATITUDE
JOURNAL

____

____

____

____

Date:
Time:
Gratitude
Journal

DATE:
TIME:
GRATITUDE JOURNAL

____

____

____

____

Date:
Time:
Gratitude
Journal

Date:
Time:
Gratitude
Journal

____

____

____

____

DATE:
TIME:
GRATITUDE JOURNAL

____

____

____

____

DATE:
TIME:
GRATITUDE
JOURNAL

____

____

____

____

DATE:
TIME:
GRATITUDE JOURNAL

DATE:
TIME:
GRATITUDE
JOURNAL

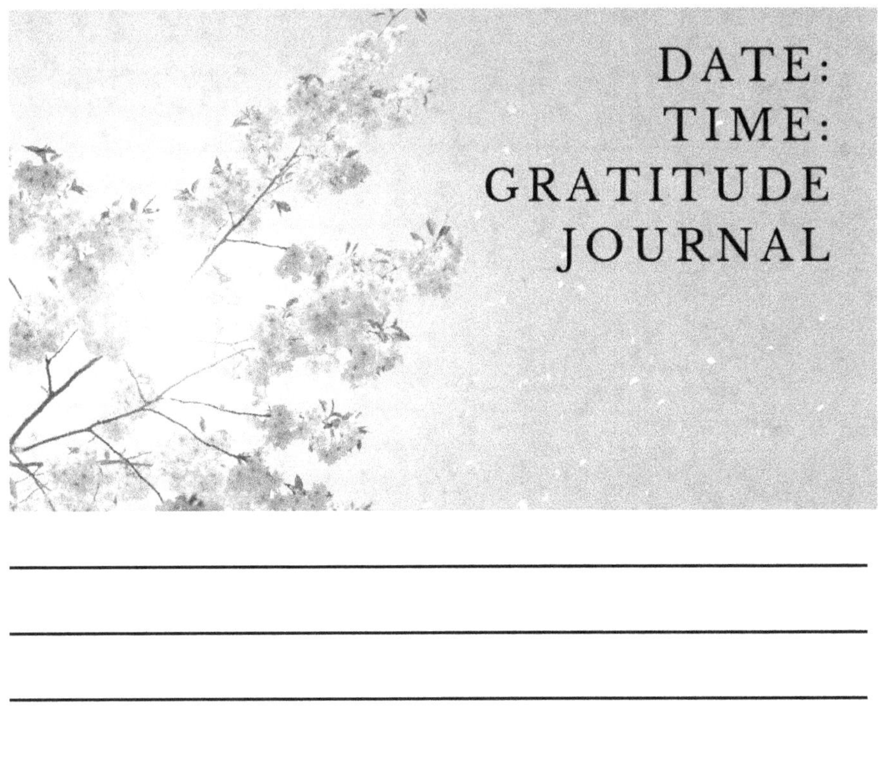
DATE:
TIME:
GRATITUDE
JOURNAL

Date:
Time:
Gratitude Journal

Date:
Time:
Gratitude Journal

____

____

____

____

Date:
Time:
Gratitude Journal

Date:
Time:
Gratitude Journal

Reflections

You are beyond worthy of love. You are beyond worthy of kindness, love, joy and peace. Surround yourself with joy and gladness. You are enough. -Joy Jallah

Your diligence will be rewarded by God. Keep holding on to the promises of God. Your labor is not in vain. —Joy Jallah

One of my happy customers Sharon ordered her copy of my published book.

www.ingramcontent.com/pod-product-compliance
Lightning Source LLC
Chambersburg PA
CBHW071344130726
47996CB00002B/822